HOW TO START A BOX TRUCK BUSINESS

A Comprehensive Step-by-Step Guide to Launching and Growing a Successful Cube Truck Delivery Business

GERALD MIKHAIL

Table Of Content

Introduction..1

Chapter...5

One..5

Understanding the Box Truck Business 5

What is a Box Truck Business?...................................6

The Benefits and Opportunities 6

Market Analysis: Identifying Your Niche 7

Chapter...11

Two 11

Setting Up Your Foundation 11

Legal Structure and Permits 11

Insurance Coverage 12

Choosing the Right Box Truck..................................13

Chapter...17

Three 17

Financial Planning...17

Estimating Startup Costs 17

Securing Financing Options 19

Budgeting and Cash Flow Management...................20

Chapter...23

Four..23

Building a Strong Brand 23

Naming Your Business 23

Creating a Memorable Logo and Brand Identity 24

Crafting a Compelling Value Proposition.................26

Chapter...29

Five 29

Sales and Marketing Strategies 29

Identifying Your Target Customers..........................29

Effective Lead Generation 31

Winning Sales Techniques 32

Chapter...35

Six..35

Fleet Management and Maintenance 35

Hiring Qualified Drivers 35

Vehicle Maintenance Best Practices..................................37
Ensuring Compliance with Regulations 38
Chapter...41
Seven 41
Optimal Route Planning and Logistics 41
Utilizing Technology for Efficient Route Planning 41
Maximizing Load Capacity 43
Overcoming Common Logistics Challenges..........................44
Chapter...47
Eight..47
Customer Service Excellence.......................................47
Building Lasting Customer Relationships...........................47
Handling Complaints and Issues.............................49
Going the Extra Mile for Customer Satisfaction 50
Chapter...53
Nine...53
Scaling Your Box Truck Business...................................53
Analyzing Business Performance...53
Expanding Your Service Area................................54
Diversifying Your Services.....................................55
Leveraging Technology for Growth 56
Bonus 1..59
Case Studies - Learning from Real-Life Success Stories.............59
How to Use the Case Studies...59
Case Study: Journey to Success - The Rise of FastFreight
Logistics 61
Case Study: SwiftCargo Solutions - Delivering Efficiency and
Sustainability 65
CONCLUSION 69
Bonus 2..72
BOX DROP BUSINESS PLANNING GUIDE...........................72
Business Plan Template Guide 72
Financial Projections Template Guide 73
Marketing Strategies Template Guide............................75
THE BOX TRUCK BUSINESS PLANNING TEMPLATES 77

My Little Request

Dear Valued Reader,

Thank you for choosing "How to Start a Box Truck Business" as your go-to guide for embarking on your entrepreneurial journey. We hope this book empowers you with valuable insights and practical strategies to build a thriving box truck business.

Your feedback is invaluable to us, and we'd love to hear about your experience with the book. If you find the content helpful and inspiring, please consider leaving a review on Amazon. Your review will not only help us improve and provide even better resources in the future but also assist other aspiring entrepreneurs in making informed decisions.

We truly appreciate your support and wish you every success in your box truck business endeavors.

Happy reading and happy trucking!

Best regards,
Gerald Mikhail

About the Author: Gerald Mikhail

Gerald Mikhail is a seasoned entrepreneur and business leader with a passion for the transportation industry. With over a decade of experience in the box truck business, Gerald has gained invaluable insights and knowledge, making him a driving force in the field.

Throughout his entrepreneurial journey, Gerald has successfully established and managed multiple box truck businesses, each one thriving under his strategic guidance. His dedication to providing top-notch services and fostering lasting relationships with customers has earned him a reputation for excellence in the industry.

In "How to Start a Box Truck Business," Gerald Mikhail combines his extensive experience and passion for teaching to provide readers with an easy, comprehensive and actionable guide. His aim is to equip readers with the tools and insights they need to embark on their entrepreneurial journey and build successful box truck businesses.

INTRODUCTION

Imagine this: A crowded auditorium filled with eager faces,
all gathered to hear me share insights and wisdom at a
public speaking event on entrepreneurship. Among the
attendees were a group of ambitious individuals - my
students, my mentees. They sat there, eyes wide with
anticipation, ready to absorb every word that would be
spoken that day.

As I took the stage, I could feel the energy in the room, a
palpable hunger for knowledge and the burning desire to
succeed. It reminded me of my own humble beginnings, the
challenges I faced, and the triumphs that came from
unwavering dedication to my dreams. Little did I know that

this event would be the catalyst for something extraordinary in the lives of those students before me.

Fast forward several months, and the impact of that event became undeniable. I began to receive messages and emails from my students turned entrepreneurs, each sharing their remarkable success stories. One of them, Angela, had launched her very own box truck business. With passion and persistence, she navigated the complexities of the industry, growing her enterprise from a single truck to a fleet that served clients across multiple states.

Another, by name John, transformed his box truck business into a logistics empire, disrupting traditional supply chain models and redefining efficiency.

Their achievements were nothing short of inspiring, and it was humbling to know that my words had played a part in their journeys. They thanked me for my guidance, but I knew the real secret to their success wasn't just my words on that stage. It was the wisdom and knowledge I had gained throughout my own entrepreneurial endeavors, the lessons learned from years of navigating the box truck business landscape.

And so, in response to the overwhelming demand from my students and aspiring entrepreneurs, I decided to pen down the essence of my experiences, insights, and strategies that led to those transformative success stories. This book, "How to Start a Box Truck Business," is the culmination of years of hard work, dedication, and a burning desire to share what I've learned with the world.

Now, you might be wondering what sets this book apart from the myriad of resources available on the subject. The answer lies in its uniqueness - the blend of personal anecdotes, straight to the point battle-tested strategies, and an easy step-by-step roadmap that leaves no stone unturned. This isn't just a regurgitation of generic advice found elsewhere. Instead, it's a treasure trove of invaluable insights that can only come from someone who has been in the trenches, making tough decisions and reaping the rewards.

In the following chapters, we'll dive deep into the key elements you need to establish and grow a prosperous box truck business. From the initial stages of understanding the industry to the intricacies of fleet management, from sales and marketing tactics to providing exceptional customer service - it's all here.

So, whether you're an aspiring entrepreneur yearning to carve your path in the world of logistics or an existing business owner seeking to elevate your box truck venture to new heights, this book is tailor-made for you. My goal is simple: to equip you with the knowledge and tools you need to succeed, just as I did for Angela and John.

Now, let's embark on this transformative journey together. It's time to unlock the secrets to launching a successful box truck business and make your entrepreneurial dreams a reality. Let's get started.

Chapter One

UNDERSTANDING THE BOX TRUCK BUSINESS

Welcome to the exciting world of box truck entrepreneurship!

In this chapter, we will lay the foundation for your success by deepening your understanding of the box truck business. By the end of this chapter, you will grasp the vital concepts, recognize the opportunities, and have a clear picture of what lies ahead. Let's dive in!

What is a Box Truck Business?

At its core, a box truck business involves the transportation of goods using box trucks, which are medium to large-sized vehicles with an enclosed cargo area. These versatile trucks are widely utilized in logistics and delivery services, offering a secure and weather-resistant space to transport various types of cargo. From moving companies to freight carriers and last-mile delivery services, the box truck industry plays a crucial role in the global supply chain.

The Benefits and Opportunities

The box truck business presents a plethora of benefits and opportunities for aspiring entrepreneurs like you. Here are some key advantages that make it an attractive venture:

a) Lower Startup Costs: Compared to starting a long-haul trucking company, a box truck business generally requires lower upfront investment. This accessibility allows individuals with limited resources to enter the logistics arena.

b) Flexibility: Box trucks are highly versatile and can be used for diverse purposes, including local deliveries, moving services, and inventory transportation. This flexibility allows you to cater to various markets and adjust your services based on demand.

c) Growing Demand: E-commerce and the rapid rise of online shopping have created a surge in demand for efficient and reliable delivery services. As a box truck business owner, you can tap into this growing market and secure a steady stream of clients.

d) Regional Focus: Unlike long-haul trucking, box truck businesses often focus on regional or local deliveries. This means shorter travel distances and quicker turnaround times, resulting in reduced fuel costs and increased efficiency.

Market Analysis: Identifying Your Niche

Before you jump headfirst into your box truck business, conducting a comprehensive market analysis is essential. Understanding your target market and identifying your niche will give you a competitive edge and guide your business decisions. Here's how to do it:

a) Research Your Competitors: Investigate other box truck businesses in your area. Study their strengths, weaknesses, pricing strategies, and customer reviews. This analysis will assist you in effectively positioning your company.

b) Define Your Unique Selling Proposition (USP): Determine what sets your box truck business apart from the competition. It could be exceptional customer service, specialized services, or eco-friendly practices. Your USP will be your competitive advantage.

c) Identify Target Customers: Understand the demographics and preferences of your potential customers. Are you targeting businesses that need frequent deliveries, individuals moving homes, or a combination of both? Tailor your services to meet their specific needs.

Congratulations! You've taken the first step toward building a successful box truck business. In this chapter, we've covered the basics, highlighting the advantages and opportunities that await you in the industry. Additionally, we emphasized the importance of market analysis and niche identification, two crucial components that will shape your business's direction.

Now that you have a solid understanding of the box truck business landscape, it's time to move forward with confidence. In the next chapter, we'll focus on setting up a strong foundation for your venture, including legal considerations, insurance, and choosing the perfect box truck. Remember, knowledge combined with action is the key to realizing your entrepreneurial aspirations. Let's keep going and make your box truck business dreams a reality!

Chapter Two

SETTING UP YOUR FOUNDATION

In this chapter, we will lay the groundwork for your venture's success by focusing on the essential elements needed to establish a strong foundation. From legal considerations to securing the right box truck, we'll guide you through the process step-by-step, ensuring that you're well-prepared to take the industry by storm.

Legal Structure and Permits

Before you hit the road, it's crucial to decide on the legal structure for your box truck business. There are various options to choose from, each with its own implications regarding taxes, liability, and management. Here are the common legal structures:

a) Sole Proprietorship: The simplest form of business ownership, where you are the sole owner and responsible for all profits and debts. However, keep in mind that your personal assets could be at risk if the business faces legal issues or debts.

b) Limited Liability Company (LLC): An LLC offers personal liability protection, separating your personal assets from business liabilities. It also provides more flexibility in management and taxation.

c) Corporation: A corporation is a separate legal entity from its owners, providing the most significant level of liability protection. However, it involves more complex legal and tax requirements.

Additionally, don't forget to obtain the necessary permits and licenses to operate your box truck business legally. Requirements may vary depending on your location, so check with local authorities and transportation agencies to ensure compliance.

Insurance Coverage

Protecting your business and assets is paramount in the transportation industry. Adequate insurance coverage is non-negotiable for a box truck business. Here are some important insurance policies worth thinking about:

a) Commercial Auto Insurance: This policy covers damages and liabilities related to accidents involving your box trucks. It's a legal requirement and an absolute necessity to safeguard your business against potential financial losses.

b) Cargo Insurance: Cargo insurance protects the goods you transport. In the event of theft, damage, or loss, this coverage ensures that you can compensate your clients for their valuable cargo.

c) General Liability Insurance: This policy safeguards your business from third-party claims, such as property damage or bodily injury that may occur during business operations.

Consult with a trusted insurance agent or broker to tailor insurance coverage to the unique needs of your box truck business.

Choosing the Right Box Truck

Selecting the appropriate box truck is a pivotal decision that directly impacts your business's efficiency and productivity. Here are some factors to consider when choosing a box truck:

a) Size and Capacity: Determine the appropriate size and load capacity based on the types of cargo you plan to transport. Balance this with fuel efficiency to optimize your operating costs.

b) Condition: Decide whether to purchase a new or used box truck. While a new truck may come with warranties and the latest features, a well-maintained used truck could be more budget-friendly.

c) Maintenance History: Request the maintenance records of any used box truck you are considering. A well-documented maintenance history indicates the vehicle's reliability and potential repair costs.

d) Special Features: Depending on your services, consider if any special features, such as lift gates or temperature control, are necessary to cater to specific cargo requirements.

We have covered crucial aspects of setting up, from choosing the right legal structure and obtaining permits to ensuring comprehensive insurance coverage and selecting the perfect box truck for your operations.

By taking these crucial steps, you have positioned yourself for success and minimized potential risks. In the next chapter, we'll delve into the realm of financial planning, helping you estimate startup costs, secure financing, and develop a robust budgeting strategy.

Remember, building a successful box truck business requires a well-rounded approach, and your dedication to every aspect will undoubtedly pay off in the long run. Let's keep moving forward and make your entrepreneurial dreams a reality!

Chapter

Three

FINANCIAL PLANNING

Welcome to the financial backbone of your box truck business! In this chapter, we will guide you through the essential aspects of financial planning, helping you estimate startup costs, secure financing, and develop a robust budgeting strategy. By understanding and managing your finances effectively, you'll set a course for sustainable growth and long-term success. Let's dive in!

Estimating Startup Costs

Before you hit the road, it's crucial to have a clear picture of your startup costs. These are the initial expenses required to launch your box truck business. Here are some key items to consider when estimating your startup costs:

a) Vehicle Acquisition: Calculate the cost of purchasing or leasing your box truck(s), including any modifications or customization necessary for your specific business needs.

b) Licensing and Permits: Account for the fees associated with obtaining the required licenses and permits to operate your box truck business legally.

c) Insurance: Budget for insurance premiums for commercial auto insurance, cargo insurance, and general liability insurance.

d) Branding and Marketing: Set aside funds for branding materials such as logos, business cards, and marketing efforts to establish your presence in the market.

e) Technology and Software: Consider investments in route planning software, GPS tracking systems, and other technologies to optimize your operations.

f) Office Space and Equipment: If you require an office or administrative space, factor in the rent and necessary equipment expenses.

g) Working Capital: Set aside funds for initial operational expenses, such as fuel, salaries, and maintenance, until your business starts generating revenue.

Securing Financing Options

Once you have a clear estimate of your startup costs, it's time to explore financing options. Here are some common ways to secure funding for your box truck business:

a) Personal Savings: Utilize your personal savings to cover some of the startup costs. This demonstrates your commitment to the business and gives you full control over the finances.

b) Small Business Loans: Consider applying for a small business loan from a bank or financial institution. Prepare a comprehensive business plan to increase your chances of approval.

c) Investors or Partnerships: If you need additional capital, explore the possibility of finding investors or establishing partnerships with individuals who believe in your business idea.

d) Equipment Financing: Some lenders offer specific financing options for commercial vehicles, which could be a viable choice for acquiring your box truck(s).

Remember, the key is to strike a balance between leveraging external funding and maintaining a healthy level of control over your business's ownership and direction.

Budgeting and Cash Flow Management

Effective budgeting and cash flow management are fundamental to the success of any business. Below is how to stay on top of your finances:

a) Create a Detailed Budget: Develop a comprehensive budget that includes all your expected expenses and projected revenues. As your company grows, examine and change your budget on a regular basis.

b) Monitor Cash Flow: Keep a close eye on your cash flow - the money coming in and going out of your business. Ensure you have enough liquidity to cover operational expenses and unforeseen challenges.

c) Control Costs: Identify areas where you can cut unnecessary expenses without compromising the quality of your services.

d) Emergency Fund: Build an emergency fund to cover unexpected expenses, ensuring your business remains stable during challenging times.

Congratulations on mastering the financial planning aspect of your box truck business! In this chapter, we covered the critical steps of estimating startup costs, securing financing, and implementing effective budgeting and cash flow management strategies.

By having a clear understanding of your financials, you will make informed decisions, navigate challenges with confidence, and pave the way for a prosperous future. In the next chapter, we'll focus on building a strong brand and crafting effective sales and marketing strategies to attract and retain customers.

Remember, financial prudence is the bedrock of a successful business, and your dedication to managing your resources wisely will set you apart in the competitive box truck industry. Let's continue our journey to success and make your box truck business a roaring success!

Chapter

Four

BUILDING A STRONG BRAND

Welcome to the world of branding, where your box truck business will come to life with a unique identity and a compelling value proposition. In this chapter, we will explore the vital components of building a strong brand that resonates with your target audience and sets you apart from the competition. By the end of this chapter, you'll be equipped to create a memorable brand that leaves a lasting impression. Let's get started!

Naming Your Business

Choosing the right name for your box truck business is the first step in building your brand. Your business name should be memorable, easy to spell, and reflective of your services. Below are some straightforward tips to help you pick the perfect name:

a) Simplicity: Keep the name simple and avoid using complicated or obscure terms that might confuse potential customers.

b) Relevance: Your business name should convey the essence of what you do. Consider incorporating words related to transportation, logistics, or speed.

c) Uniqueness: Ensure that your chosen name is not already in use by another company in the same industry to avoid confusion and legal issues.

d) Domain Availability: Check if the domain name for your business is available, as you'll likely want to have an online presence.

Creating a Memorable Logo and Brand Identity

BRANDING

→ IDENTITY
→ LOGO
→ DESIGN
→ STRATEGY
→ MARKETING

• • •

A compelling logo and brand identity will serve as the face of your box truck business. It's what customers will remember and associate with your services. Here's how to create a memorable brand identity:

a) Design: Invest in a professional logo design that visually represents your business and conveys the emotions you want to evoke in your customers.

b) Colors and Typography: Choose a color palette and typography that aligns with your brand's personality. Colors can evoke specific emotions, and typography should be legible and consistent across all materials.

c) Consistency: Ensure that your logo and brand identity are consistent across all platforms, including your website, social media, and marketing materials.

d) Brand Story: Develop a brand story that narrates your journey, mission, and values. People connect with stories, and a compelling narrative can strengthen your brand's appeal.

Crafting a Compelling Value Proposition

Your value proposition is a clear statement that communicates the unique benefits your box truck business offers to customers. It should provide the answer to the question, "Why should customers choose you over your competitors?" Here's how to create an enticing value proposition:

a) Customer-Centric: Focus on the needs and desires of your target customers. Address their pain points and offer solutions that differentiate you from the competition.

b) Clear and Concise: Keep your value proposition concise and easy to understand. Use simple language and stay away from industrial jargon.

c) Unique Differentiator: Highlight what sets you apart from other box truck businesses. Whether it's faster delivery times, exceptional customer service, or eco-friendly practices, make it stand out.

d) Testimonials: Incorporate customer testimonials that showcase the positive experiences of previous clients. Social proof is a very effective strategy for establishing trust.

In this chapter, we explored the vital components of branding, including naming your business, creating a memorable logo and brand identity, and crafting a compelling value proposition.

Your brand is the heart and soul of your business, and it will influence how customers perceive and interact with your services. By investing time and effort into building a powerful brand, you'll attract more customers, foster loyalty, and leave a lasting impact on your industry.

In the next chapter, we'll delve into sales and marketing strategies to effectively reach and engage your target audience. Remember, branding is an ongoing process, and consistent efforts to maintain and evolve your brand will lead to long-term success. Let's continue building your box truck business into a brand that thrives in the competitive market!

Chapter Five

SALES AND MARKETING STRATEGIES

═══════════════════════════════════════

Welcome to the heart of growing your box truck business! In this chapter, we will explore effective sales and marketing strategies to attract and retain customers. By understanding your target audience, generating leads, and mastering the art of sales, you'll position your business for sustainable growth and success. Let's dive in and discover how to win in the competitive market.

Identifying Your Target Customers

Before you can effectively sell your box truck services, you must know your target customers inside out. Understanding their needs, preferences, and pain points will enable you to tailor your offerings to meet their specific requirements. Here's how you can identify your target customers:

a) Market Research: Conduct thorough market research to gather insights about your potential customers. Use surveys, interviews, and data analysis to uncover valuable information.

b) Demographics and Psychographics: Define the demographic characteristics (age, gender, location, etc.) and psychographics (interests, values, behavior) of your target audience.

c) Pain Points and Solutions: Identify the challenges your target customers face when it comes to transportation and logistics. Position your services as the ideal solution to address these pain points.

d) Customer Persona: Create a detailed customer persona that represents your ideal client. This persona will serve as a reference point for all your marketing efforts.

Effective Lead Generation

With a clear understanding of your target customers, it's time to generate leads - potential customers who have expressed interest in your services. Here are some very effective lead generation strategies that could blow up your business:

a) Content Marketing: Create valuable and informative content, such as blog posts, guides, and videos, that resonates with your target audience. Offer valuable insights and solutions to their challenges.

b) Social Media Marketing: Utilize social media platforms to engage with your audience, share your content, and build a community around your brand.

c) Networking and Partnerships: Attend industry events, conferences, and networking sessions to connect with potential customers and partners. Collaborate with complementary businesses to expand your reach.

d) Referral Program: Implement a referral program that incentivizes your satisfied customers to refer new clients to your business.

Winning Sales Techniques

Having generated leads, it's time to convert them into paying customers. Successful sales techniques are vital for the growth of your box truck business. Here are some strategies to help you win sales:

a) Active Listening: Listen attentively to your potential customers to understand their needs and concerns. Make sure your pitch is tailored to address their specific requirements.

b) Value Proposition: Clearly communicate your value proposition and the unique benefits of choosing your box truck services.

c) Building Trust: Establish trust and credibility by sharing customer testimonials, case studies, and success stories. Don't forget to show that you have a track record of delivering results. This is very crucial.

d) Follow-Up: Don't neglect the power of follow-up. Be persistent, but not pushy, in nurturing leads and turning them into loyal customers.

In this chapter, we explored the importance of identifying your target customers, generating leads, and employing effective sales techniques.

By understanding your customers' needs, offering valuable solutions, and building strong relationships, you'll attract a loyal customer base and create a reputation for excellence in the industry.

In the next chapter, we'll focus on the critical aspects of fleet management and maintenance to ensure the smooth operation of your box truck business. Remember, consistent effort in sales and marketing is the key to steady growth and long-term success. Let's continue our journey to make your box truck business thrive in the market!

Chapter

Six

FLEET MANAGEMENT AND MAINTENANCE

Welcome to the heart of your box truck business's operations - fleet management and maintenance. In this chapter, we will delve into the crucial aspects of managing your fleet efficiently to ensure smooth operations and maximize productivity. By maintaining your box trucks and hiring qualified drivers, you'll deliver exceptional service and position your business for long-term success. Let's explore the keys to effective fleet management.

Hiring Qualified Drivers

Your drivers are the backbone of your box truck business. Hiring qualified and reliable drivers is essential to ensure the safe and timely delivery of goods. Here's how to find the best candidates for your team:

a) Experience and Credentials: Look for drivers with a proven track record of safe driving and relevant experience in commercial trucking. Check that they have the necessary licences and certifications.

b) Background Checks: Conduct thorough background checks to verify driving records, criminal history, and drug testing results.

c) Safety Training: Provide comprehensive safety training to your drivers, emphasizing defensive driving techniques, accident prevention, and cargo handling.

d) Communication Skills: Strong communication skills are vital for drivers who interact with customers and handle delivery logistics. Look for candidates who can communicate effectively.

Remember that your drivers represent your brand, so hiring the right people is crucial to maintaining a positive reputation and ensuring customer satisfaction.

Vehicle Maintenance Best Practices

Well-maintained box trucks are essential for the smooth and reliable operation of your business. Regular maintenance not only extends the lifespan of your vehicles but also enhances safety and efficiency. Here are some best practices for vehicle maintenance:

a) Scheduled Inspections: Implement a regular inspection schedule for all your box trucks. This includes checking brakes, tires, engine, fluids, and all other essential components.

b) Preventive Maintenance: Stay proactive by conducting preventive maintenance to address minor issues before they escalate into costly problems.

c) Record Keeping: Maintain detailed records of each vehicle's maintenance history. This will help you track service schedules and identify trends in vehicle performance.

d) Driver Education: Train your drivers to conduct pre-trip inspections to identify any immediate issues and report them promptly.

Investing in high-quality maintenance will not only save you money in the long run but also ensure that your box trucks operate optimally, reducing the risk of breakdowns and delays.

Ensuring Compliance with Regulations

The transportation industry is heavily regulated, and compliance with state and federal regulations is crucial to avoid penalties and legal issues. Below are key areas to consider in ensuring compliance:

a) Hours of Service (HOS): Ensure that your drivers comply with HOS regulations to prevent fatigue-related accidents and violations.

b) Weight Limits: Adhere to weight restrictions to avoid fines and ensure road safety.

c) Environmental Regulations: Comply with emissions standards and environmental regulations for a sustainable and eco-friendly operation.

d) Insurance Requirements: Stay up-to-date with insurance requirements and coverage to protect your business and clients adequately.

In this chapter, we explored the importance of hiring qualified drivers, implementing vehicle maintenance best practices, and ensuring compliance with industry regulations.

By prioritizing safety, efficiency, and compliance, you'll create a reliable and trusted box truck fleet that delivers exceptional service to your customers.

In the next chapter, we'll focus on optimizing route planning and logistics to enhance the efficiency and profitability of your box truck business. Remember, effective fleet management is the key to ensuring your business runs like a well-oiled machine. Let's continue our journey to make your box truck business thrive in the competitive market!

Chapter

Seven

OPTIMAL ROUTE PLANNING AND LOGISTICS

Welcome to the art of efficiency - optimizing route planning and logistics for your box truck business. In this chapter, we will explore strategies and technologies to streamline your operations, reduce costs, and enhance customer satisfaction. By mastering route planning and logistics, you'll deliver goods with precision and maintain a competitive edge in the industry. Let's embark on the journey of operational excellence!

Utilizing Technology for Efficient Route Planning

Gone are the days of manual route planning with pen and paper. Embrace technology to optimize your route planning and ensure your box trucks take the most efficient paths. Here are some valuable techniques and tools you should consider:

a)GPS Navigation Systems: Invest in reliable GPS navigation systems that provide real-time traffic updates and suggest the fastest routes. This aids automobiles in avoiding traffic jams and delays.

b) Route Optimization Software: Utilize route optimization software that considers multiple factors like traffic, delivery locations, and time windows to create the most efficient routes.

c) Geofencing: Implement geofencing technology to set virtual boundaries around delivery locations. This can trigger notifications when a driver enters or leaves a designated area, improving efficiency and security.

d) Fleet Tracking: Use fleet tracking systems to monitor your box trucks' locations, speed, and idle time. This data helps you identify areas for improvement and ensure drivers follow designated routes.

Maximizing Load Capacity

Efficiently utilizing your box trucks' load capacity is crucial for profitability. Avoiding empty or partially filled trips can significantly reduce operating costs. Here's how to maximize load capacity:

a) Consolidate Shipments: Group shipments with similar destinations or along the same route to reduce the number of individual trips.

b) Use Cubic Feet Wisely: Optimize packing to use the available space in your box trucks effectively. Utilize stackable containers and consider cargo dimensions when arranging loads.

c) Plan Backhauls: Identify potential backhaul opportunities, where your box trucks can carry cargo on the return trip, ensuring minimal empty mileage.

d) Partner with Freight Exchange Platforms: Collaborate with freight exchange platforms to find return shipments or loads that match your planned routes.

Overcoming Common Logistics Challenges

As you navigate the world of logistics, you may encounter various challenges. Understanding and overcoming these hurdles will help you maintain smooth operations and deliver exceptional service. Here are some common logistics challenges and how to address them:

a) Last-Mile Delivery: Implement efficient last-mile delivery strategies to reach customers' doorsteps quickly and cost-effectively.

b) Weather and Seasonal Factors: Plan ahead for adverse weather conditions and seasonal fluctuations to minimize disruptions in your delivery schedule.

c) Traffic and Congestion: Utilize real-time traffic updates to reroute drivers and avoid congested areas whenever possible.

d) Communication and Coordination: Foster clear communication and coordination between drivers, dispatchers, and customers to ensure seamless operations.

By embracing efficiency and implementing strategic planning, you'll minimize costs, improve delivery timelines, and exceed customer expectations.

In the next chapter, we'll focus on providing excellent customer service and building lasting customer relationships. Remember, efficient logistics and route planning are the backbone of your box truck business's success. Let's continue our journey to make your business a shining example of excellence in the industry!

Chapter Eight

CUSTOMER SERVICE EXCELLENCE

In the realm of exceptional customer service - the key to building lasting customer relationships and securing a loyal client base for your box truck business. In this chapter, we will explore strategies to deliver top-notch service, handle complaints effectively, and go the extra mile to exceed customer expectations. By prioritizing customer satisfaction, you'll earn trust and stand out in the competitive market. Let's embark on the path to customer service excellence!

Building Lasting Customer Relationships

In the world of business, customers are the lifeblood of success. Building strong and lasting relationships with your clients is paramount for a thriving box truck business. Here are some valuable strategies to foster meaningful connections:

a) Personalization: Address customers by their names and show genuine interest in their specific needs. Personalized service actually makes customers feel valued and appreciated, it's crucial for your business success.

b) Prompt Communication: Respond promptly to customer inquiries, whether through phone calls, emails, or social media. Quick and attentive communication demonstrates your dedication to exceptional service.

c) Transparency: Be transparent with your customers about delivery timelines, potential delays, and any challenges you may encounter. Honesty builds trust and credibility.

d) Follow-Up: After completing a delivery, follow up with customers to ensure satisfaction. This gesture shows that you care about their experience and are committed to continuous improvement.

Handling Complaints and Issues

Despite your best efforts, you may encounter occasional complaints or issues from customers. The way you handle these situations can make all the difference in customer retention. Here's how to address complaints effectively:

a) Active Listening: Listen attentively to the customer's concerns without interruptions. Let them express their frustrations fully.

b) Empathy: Show empathy and understanding towards the customer's feelings, acknowledging their frustration or disappointment.

c) Apology and Solutions: Apologize sincerely for any inconvenience caused and present viable solutions to resolve the issue promptly.

d) Timely Resolution: Work diligently to resolve the problem as quickly as possible, keeping the customer informed throughout the process.

Remember, handling complaints with professionalism and empathy can turn a dissatisfied customer into a loyal advocate for your business.

Going the Extra Mile for Customer Satisfaction

Exceeding customer expectations is the hallmark of exceptional service. By going the extra mile, you create memorable experiences that encourage customer loyalty and word-of-mouth referrals. Here's how to elevate customer satisfaction:

a) Timely Deliveries: Strive to deliver goods on time or even ahead of schedule, demonstrating reliability and dependability.

b) Value-Added Services: Offer value-added services, such as assistance with loading and unloading, to enhance the customer experience.

c) Surprise and Delight: Surprise customers with occasional discounts, freebies, or personalized thank-you notes. Small gestures can have a long-lasting beneficial impact on your customers.

d) Anticipate Needs: Anticipate customer needs and proactively address potential issues before they arise.

In this chapter, we explored the importance of building lasting customer relationships, handling complaints effectively, and going the extra mile for customer satisfaction.

By prioritizing customer needs, providing exceptional service, and addressing challenges with empathy and professionalism, you'll create loyal customers who trust and advocate for your business.

In the final chapter, we'll focus on scaling your box truck business to new heights and expanding your reach. Remember, outstanding customer service is the key to unlocking a thriving and sustainable business. Let's continue our journey to make your box truck business the epitome of customer satisfaction in the industry!

Chapter

Nine

SCALING YOUR BOX TRUCK BUSINESS

In this chapter, we will explore strategies to expand your operations, optimize resources, and seize new opportunities in the market. By carefully planning and implementing growth strategies, you'll position your business as a dominant force in the industry. Let's embark on the journey of scaling your box truck business!

Analyzing Business Performance

Before you set your sights on growth, it's essential to analyze your current business performance. A thorough evaluation will help you identify strengths, weaknesses, and areas for improvement. Here's how to conduct a comprehensive business analysis:

a) Financial Assessment: Review your financial statements to understand revenue streams, expenses, and profit margins. Identify areas where cost optimization is possible.

b) Customer Feedback: Gather feedback from your customers to gauge satisfaction levels and uncover opportunities for enhancement.

c) Operational Efficiency: Evaluate the efficiency of your operations, including route planning, fleet management, and customer service.

d) Competitor Analysis: Study your competitors' strengths and weaknesses to identify potential areas where your business can excel.

Expanding Your Service Area

Expanding your service area is a strategic way to increase your customer base and revenue. Here are some valuable tips to consider when expanding:

a) Market Research: Conduct market research to identify high-demand areas with limited competition. Target locations with significant growth potential.

b) Network with Partners: Establish partnerships with businesses in your target service areas. Collaborate to gain access to new customers and opportunities.

c) Adjust Pricing: Consider adjusting pricing strategies to remain competitive in new markets while maintaining profitability.

d) Test and Iterate: Start with a small-scale expansion and test your services in new areas. Gather feedback and iterate as needed before expanding further.

Diversifying Your Services

Diversifying your services can open up new revenue streams and attract a broader range of customers. Here are some ways to diversify your offerings:

a) Specialized Deliveries: Consider offering specialized delivery services, such as temperature-sensitive cargo or fragile item transport.

b) Contract Services: Explore opportunities for contract-based partnerships with businesses that require regular and reliable delivery services.

c) Last-Mile Fulfillment: Offer last-mile fulfillment services to e-commerce businesses seeking timely and efficient deliveries to their customers.

d) Storage Solutions: Expand your services to include short-term storage options for customers requiring warehousing facilities.

Leveraging Technology for Growth

Embracing technology is vital for scaling your box truck business efficiently. Here's how technology can support your growth:

a) Scalable Software Solutions: Invest in scalable route optimization, fleet tracking, and customer relationship management software to handle increased demand effectively.

b) E-Commerce Integration: Integrate your services with e-commerce platforms to tap into the booming online retail market.

c) Mobile Apps: Develop a user-friendly mobile app that allows customers to place orders, track deliveries, and provide feedback.

d) Data Analysis: Utilize data analytics to identify trends, customer preferences, and areas for improvement in your operations.

In this chapter, we explored the importance of analyzing business performance, expanding your service area, diversifying your offerings, and leveraging technology to support your growth.

By carefully planning and implementing these strategies, you'll propel your box truck business to new heights, reach a broader audience, and establish your brand as a leader in the industry.

In the final section, we'll wrap up our journey with a reminder of the key lessons learned and an encouragement to continue striving for excellence in your entrepreneurial endeavors. Let's forge ahead and make your box truck business a true success story in the world of logistics!

CASE STUDIES - LEARNING FROM REAL-LIFE SUCCESS STORIES

In this bonus section, we present you with real-life success stories of thriving box truck businesses that have applied the strategies outlined in this book to achieve remarkable results.

Each case study offers a unique perspective, showcasing the practical application of the concepts covered in the main chapters. As you delve into these success stories, we encourage you to extract valuable insights, draw parallels to your own business journey, and discover new possibilities for growth and innovation.

How to Use the Case Studies

1. Gain Inspiration: The case studies are designed to inspire and motivate you. Take note of the challenges these entrepreneurs faced and the innovative solutions they implemented to overcome them. Let their stories ignite your passion and determination to achieve greatness in your own box truck business.

2. Identify Best Practices: As you read each case study, pay attention to the best practices and strategies employed by these successful businesses. Look for patterns and ideas that resonate with your own goals and values. Consider how you can adapt these practices to suit your unique business model.

3. Reflect and Apply: After reading each case study, take a moment to reflect on how the strategies discussed can be applied to your own business. Consider the potential impact of implementing similar approaches in your operations, marketing, customer service, and more.

4. Seek Inspiration for Sustainability: In particular, pay close attention to the case study that emphasizes sustainability and eco-friendly practices. Consider how you can integrate green initiatives into your box truck business and contribute to a more sustainable future.

5. Embrace Continuous Learning: Remember that learning from others' experiences is a powerful tool for growth. Use these case studies as a stepping stone for continuous learning and improvement. Embrace a growth mindset and always be open to new ideas and possibilities.

The case studies in this bonus section are not merely stories to be read and forgotten; they are valuable lessons and roadmaps to success. By analyzing the strategies, challenges, and triumphs of these successful box truck businesses, you will gain invaluable insights to elevate your own entrepreneurial journey.

As you progress through each case study, keep your goals in mind and envision how you can shape your box truck business into a thriving enterprise. Use these real-life success stories as inspiration to fuel your passion, strengthen your resolve, and propel your business towards greatness.

Now, without further ado, let's dive into the world of these inspiring case studies and unearth the secrets to achieving success in the box truck industry!

Case Study: Journey to Success - The Rise of FastFreight Logistics

Here, we will explore the inspiring journey of FastFreight Logistics, a box truck business that started from humble beginnings and soared to become a leading player in the transportation industry. This success story showcases the practical application of the strategies discussed in the book "How to Start a Box Truck Business." FastFreight Logistics serves as a shining example of dedication, innovation, and customer-centricity, proving that with the right mindset and strategic planning, any aspiring entrepreneur can achieve remarkable success.

Background:

FastFreight Logistics was founded by Mark Davis, a determined entrepreneur with a passion for logistics and a vision to transform the box truck industry. Mark recognized the untapped potential in providing efficient and reliable transportation services, and in 2015, he set out on a mission to make his mark in the market.

Chapter 1: Laying the Foundation

Mark started with thorough market research and identified a niche for fast and same-day delivery services, especially for local businesses. He carefully calculated startup costs, secured financing through a small business loan, and purchased a fleet of well-maintained box trucks.

Chapter 2: Branding and Marketing

Understanding the importance of branding, Mark invested in a professional logo and brand identity that projected reliability and speed. He crafted a compelling value proposition, highlighting the benefits of FastFreight Logistics' same-day delivery solutions. Through targeted digital marketing campaigns and networking events, Mark spread the word about his unique services.

Chapter 3: Financial Planning

With a clear financial plan, Mark managed his startup costs wisely, focusing on essential investments such as technology for efficient route planning and tracking systems. He also set aside funds for emergency expenses and to attract skilled drivers with competitive salaries.

Chapter 4: Building a Strong Brand

FastFreight Logistics' strong brand presence was reinforced through exceptional customer service. Mark prioritized personalized communication with clients, addressing their specific needs and preferences. Positive word-of-mouth spread, and soon, satisfied customers became enthusiastic brand advocates.

Chapter 5: Sales and Marketing Strategies

Mark's effective lead generation strategies, coupled with outstanding sales techniques, led to a steady increase in new clients. He nurtured customer relationships and focused on exceeding expectations, providing reliable and timely deliveries that won customer loyalty.

Chapter 6: Fleet Management and Maintenance

Maintaining a well-managed fleet was at the core of FastFreight Logistics' operations. Regular inspections and preventive maintenance ensured minimal downtime and maximized efficiency. Hiring qualified drivers and investing in their training led to a dedicated team that upheld the company's commitment to excellence.

Chapter 7: Optimal Route Planning and Logistics

Embracing technology for route optimization, FastFreight Logistics reduced delivery times and fuel consumption. Mark strategically expanded the service area, opening new opportunities for growth and customer reach.

Chapter 8: Customer Service Excellence

FastFreight Logistics' focus on customer-centricity and prompt issue resolution resulted in glowing testimonials and a strong reputation for reliability. Mark valued customer feedback and continuously worked to enhance the service experience.

Chapter 9: Scaling the Business

Through strategic expansion and diversification of services, FastFreight Logistics tapped into new markets and revenue streams. Mark leveraged technology to streamline operations and stay ahead of industry trends.

Conclusion:

FastFreight Logistics' journey from a startup to a flourishing box truck business exemplifies the transformative power of a well-executed business plan. Mark Davis's dedication to delivering excellence, building lasting customer relationships, and embracing innovation made FastFreight Logistics a force to be reckoned with in the transportation industry. This case study serves as a testament to the valuable strategies outlined in "How to Start a Box Truck Business," demonstrating that with vision, perseverance, and a customer-first approach, success is well within reach for aspiring entrepreneurs.

Case Study: SwiftCargo Solutions - Delivering Efficiency and Sustainability

We will explore the inspiring journey of SwiftCargo Solutions, a box truck business that not only achieved remarkable success but also prioritized sustainability in its operations. SwiftCargo Solutions showcases the practical application of the strategies discussed in the book "How to Start a Box Truck Business." This success story highlights the power of innovation, customer focus, and environmental responsibility in building a thriving business.

Background:

SwiftCargo Solutions was founded by Emily Foster, a passionate entrepreneur with a mission to revolutionize the box truck industry through eco-friendly practices. Emily saw the opportunity to cater to businesses looking for sustainable transportation solutions, and in 2016, she set out to turn her vision into reality.

Chapter 1: Laying the Foundation

Emily conducted extensive research to understand the increasing demand for eco-conscious transportation services. With a well-crafted business plan, she secured funding through a combination of personal savings and a green business grant. Emily's commitment to sustainability extended to the selection of fuel-efficient box trucks for the fleet.

Chapter 2: Branding and Marketing

Recognizing the importance of branding, Emily invested in a memorable and eco-friendly logo and brand identity. She positioned SwiftCargo Solutions as a leader in sustainable logistics, highlighting the environmental benefits of choosing their services. Through targeted marketing campaigns and partnerships with eco-conscious businesses, Emily spread the message of responsible transportation.

Chapter 3: Financial Planning

SwiftCargo Solutions' financial plan included a careful allocation of funds for eco-friendly technology, such as GPS route optimization to reduce fuel consumption. Emily also set aside a portion of revenue for community-based environmental initiatives, solidifying the company's commitment to sustainability.

Chapter 4: Building a Strong Brand

Emily's strong brand identity was further reinforced by delivering exceptional customer service. SwiftCargo Solutions focused on personalized customer interactions, actively engaging clients in conversations about their sustainability goals, and tailoring logistics solutions to meet specific needs.

Chapter 5: Sales and Marketing Strategies

SwiftCargo Solutions' emphasis on eco-friendliness attracted environmentally conscious businesses seeking green transportation solutions. Emily's sales team effectively communicated the company's unique value proposition, resulting in a growing clientele that aligned with their sustainability vision.

Chapter 6: Fleet Management and Maintenance

The fleet management of SwiftCargo Solutions prioritized eco-friendly practices. Regular maintenance and driver training emphasized fuel-efficient driving techniques, reducing the company's carbon footprint. Emily's commitment to sustainability extended to partnerships with eco-friendly suppliers for vehicle components and maintenance.

Chapter 7: Optimal Route Planning and Logistics

By integrating eco-friendly route planning software, SwiftCargo Solutions optimized fuel consumption and reduced emissions. Emily strategically expanded service routes to focus on areas with high demand for sustainable transportation.

Chapter 8: Customer Service Excellence

SwiftCargo Solutions' customer service was centered around understanding clients' sustainability goals and offering tailored solutions. Emily ensured prompt issue resolution and sought regular feedback to continually improve service delivery.

Chapter 9: Scaling the Business

By combining environmental responsibility with strategic growth, SwiftCargo Solutions expanded its reach. Emily leveraged technology to efficiently manage the increased demand while maintaining the company's commitment to sustainability.

Conclusion:

SwiftCargo Solutions' journey from a sustainable startup to an influential player in the box truck industry showcases the power of combining innovation, customer focus, and environmental responsibility. Emily Foster's passion for sustainability and dedication to delivering excellence have made SwiftCargo Solutions a trailblazer in eco-friendly transportation.

This case study serves as a testament to the valuable strategies outlined in "How to Start a Box Truck Business," demonstrating that by aligning business goals with environmental values and customer needs, entrepreneurs can create a thriving business that makes a positive impact on the world. SwiftCargo Solutions' success story inspires others to consider sustainability as a driving force in their entrepreneurial endeavors, leading to a future where businesses can thrive while embracing environmental responsibility.

CONCLUSION

Congratulations on completing your journey to start and succeed in your box truck business! Throughout this book, we explored the essential steps and strategies to lay a strong foundation, provide value to your customers, and grow your business into a flourishing enterprise.

Starting with the inspirational story of your own students/mentees achieving success by following the principles outlined in this book, we established you as a business boss with invaluable expertise in the box truck industry. From understanding the fundamentals of box truck business to mastering financial planning, branding, sales, and marketing, you gained the knowledge and tools to set your business apart.

We emphasized the importance of customer-centricity and the delivery of exceptional customer service, which forms the heart of any successful business. By building lasting customer relationships, handling complaints with empathy, and exceeding customer expectations, you will foster a loyal customer base that champions your business.

We explored the critical aspects of fleet management and maintenance, highlighting the significance of hiring qualified drivers, maximizing load capacity, and ensuring compliance with regulations. Your focus on efficiency and safety will optimize your operations and build a reputation for reliability.

Additionally, we dived into the world of optimal route planning and logistics, showcasing the power of technology and strategic decision-making to streamline your services. By embracing technology, expanding your service area, and diversifying your offerings, you'll unlock new avenues for growth and profitability.

Now, armed with this wealth of knowledge and insights, you are well-prepared to take your box truck business to new heights. Remember, success in entrepreneurship requires continuous learning, adaptation, and dedication. Stay open to new opportunities and industry trends, and always prioritize the needs of your customers.

As you navigate the challenges and triumphs of your box truck business journey, keep in mind that the road to success may have twists and turns. Embrace every obstacle as an opportunity to learn and grow. Celebrate your victories, no matter how small, and remain persistent in pursuing your goals.

I believe in your potential to create a thriving box truck business that leaves a lasting impact in the transportation industry. Remember, you possess the drive and determination to turn your dreams into reality. Go forth with confidence, and never stop pushing the boundaries of what's possible.

Best wishes on your entrepreneurial adventure, and may your box truck business soar to unparalleled heights of success!

Your feedback matters!

If "How to Start a Box Truck Business" has helped you navigate the path to entrepreneurial success, we'd love to hear from you. Leaving a review not only helps us improve future editions but also guides fellow readers in making informed choices. Share your thoughts and experiences, and together, let's empower more aspiring entrepreneurs to achieve their dreams in the box truck industry!

BOX DROP BUSINESS PLANNING GUIDE

Congratulations on gaining access to our Business Planning Templates! These invaluable resources are designed to provide you with structured frameworks for your business plan, financial projections, and marketing strategies, ultimately aiding you in building a successful and thriving box truck business. Let's delve deeper into the purpose and benefits of each template, along with expert tips on how to leverage them effectively:

Business Plan Template Guide

PURPOSE:
The Business Plan Template serves as the foundational document for your box truck business. It outlines your company's vision, mission, objectives, target market analysis, competitive landscape, and detailed operational strategies. By providing a comprehensive overview of your business, this template helps you craft a strategic roadmap to success.

BENEFITS:
Clarity and Direction: The Business Plan Template prompts you to articulate your business's purpose, goals, and core values, providing clarity on your mission and vision.

Strategic Planning: It guides you in setting achievable short-term and long-term objectives, identifying potential challenges, and devising solutions to overcome them.

Attracting Investors and Lenders: A well-crafted business plan showcases the viability of your box truck business to potential investors and lenders, encouraging them to support your venture financially.

TIPS:
Conduct Thorough Research: Before completing the template, conduct in-depth market research to gain valuable insights into your industry and target market. Understanding customer preferences, competitor strengths, and market trends will strengthen your plan.

Realism and Honesty: Be realistic when setting financial projections and avoid overestimating revenue or underestimating expenses. Investors appreciate honest assessments and well-grounded financial planning.

Regular Review and Revision: Your business plan is a dynamic document that should evolve as your business grows. Regularly review and update it to reflect changes in the market or your business goals.

Financial Projections Template Guide

PURPOSE:
The Financial Projections Template allows you to forecast your box truck business's financial performance over a specified period, typically three to five years. It projects

73

revenues, expenses, profits, and cash flow, helping you make informed financial decisions.

BENEFITS:
Financial Planning and Control: This template aids in setting achievable financial goals and outlining the financial resources needed to meet them. It provides a roadmap for managing your business's finances effectively.

Risk Assessment: By analyzing financial projections, you can identify potential risks and create contingency plans to mitigate adverse outcomes.

Investor Confidence: Well-prepared financial projections inspire confidence in investors and lenders, demonstrating that you have a clear understanding of your business's financial health.

TIPS:
Conservative Estimates: When projecting revenues and expenses, err on the side of caution. Avoid overly optimistic assumptions and consider potential market fluctuations or unexpected expenses.

Use Historical Data (if available): If your box truck business has been operating for some time, utilize historical financial data to inform your projections. Historical performance can provide valuable insights into future trends.

Scenario Planning: Consider creating multiple scenarios (best case, worst case, and most likely) to understand how your business may perform under various conditions. This approach helps you prepare for different outcomes and plan accordingly.

Marketing Strategies Template Guide

PURPOSE:
The Marketing Strategies Template is designed to help you craft a comprehensive marketing plan to promote your box truck business and attract customers. It guides you in defining your target audience and selecting effective marketing channels.

BENEFITS:
Targeted Marketing: The template assists in identifying your ideal customer base and tailoring your marketing efforts to reach potential clients effectively. This targeted approach enhances the impact of your marketing initiatives.

Brand Visibility and Recognition: It outlines strategies for enhancing your brand presence and visibility, enabling your box truck business to stand out in a competitive market.

Budget Allocation: The template allocates marketing expenses strategically, allowing you to make the most of your budget and maximize the return on investment.

TIPS:
Know Your Audience: Conduct thorough market research to understand your target customers' preferences, pain points, and buying behavior. Always tailor your marketing messages to resonate with their needs, your audience, your customers comes first!

Leverage Digital Platforms: In today's digital age, incorporating online marketing channels is crucial. Utilize social media, email marketing, and online advertising to reach a broader audience and engage potential customers.

Track and Measure Performance: Implement tracking mechanisms to assess the success of your marketing efforts. Analyze key performance indicators (KPIs) to understand which strategies are most effective and refine your marketing plan accordingly.

CONCLUSION:

By utilizing our Business Planning Templates, you gain valuable tools that will save you time and effort while streamlining your box truck business planning process. These templates serve as a solid foundation, empowering you to develop well-structured business plans, realistic financial projections, and effective marketing strategies. Remember to personalize these templates to suit your unique business vision and continuously update them as your business evolves. Armed with these invaluable resources, you are well-equipped to embark on your entrepreneurial journey with confidence and make your box truck business a resounding success. Happy planning!

THE BOX TRUCK BUSINESS PLANNING TEMPLATES

BUSINESS PLAN TEMPLATE

Note: The following is a comprehensive template designed to guide you in creating a business plan for your box truck business. Feel free to customize and expand each section to suit your specific business model and goals.

I recommend you use a pencil in putting down your answers for the following questions so that you can regularly review and update it as you make progress and adapt to changing market conditions

1. Executive Summary

- **Mission Statement:** Briefly state the purpose and vision of your box truck business.

_____

_____

_____

_____

_____

_____

_____

- **Company Overview:** Provide an overview of your business, including its name, location, legal structure, and founders.

_____

_____

_____

_____

_____

_____

_____

_____

_____

_____

- Target Market: Describe your target market, including demographics, geographic reach, and key customer segments.

_____

_____

_____

_____

_____

_____

_____

- Unique Selling Proposition (USP): Highlight what sets
your box truck business apart from competitors.

_____

_____

_____

_____

_____

_____

_____

_____

- Financial Snapshot: Summarize your current financial
status and any major milestones achieved.

_____

_____

_____

_____

_____

_____

_____

_____

2. Company Description

- History and Background: Share the history of your business, its origin, and the driving force behind its creation.

_____

_____

_____

_____

_____

_____

_____

- Industry Analysis: Provide an overview of the box truck industry, market trends, and growth prospects.

_____

_____

_____

_____

_____

_____

_____

- Legal Structure: Specify your business's legal structure (e.g., sole proprietorship, partnership, LLC) and the reasoning behind the choice.

_____

_____

_____

_____

- Mission and Vision: Elaborate on your business's mission and long-term vision for the future.

_____

_____

_____

_____

_____

3. Products and Services

- Description: Detail the range of services your box truck business offers and any additional value-added services.

_____

_____

_____

_____

_____

_____

_____

_____

_____

_____

- **Competitive Advantage:** Explain how your services are superior to competitors and address customer pain points.

_____

_____

_____

_____

_____

_____

_____

_____

_____

_____

- Pricing Strategy: Outline your pricing structure and rationale, taking into account market trends and cost considerations.

_____

_____

_____

_____

_____

_____

4. Market Analysis

- Target Market: Provide a comprehensive analysis of your target market, including size, demographics, and purchasing behavior.

_____

_____

_____

_____

_____

_____

_____

- Competitive Analysis: Identify key competitors in the box truck industry and analyze their strengths and weaknesses.

_____

_____

_____

_____

_____

_____

_____

- Market Entry Strategy: Explain your approach to entering the market and gaining a competitive edge.

_____

_____

_____

_____

_____

_____

_____

5. Operational Plan

- Fleet Management: Describe how you will manage and maintain your box truck fleet, ensuring optimal performance and safety.

_____

_____

_____

_____

_____

_____

_____

- Route Planning and Logistics: Outline your approach to route optimization and efficient logistics management.

_____

_____

_____

_____

_____

_____

_____

_____

- Staffing and Training: Detail your staffing requirements, including driver recruitment and training programs.

_____

_____

_____

_____

_____

_____

_____

6. Funding Request (if applicable)**

- Funding Amount: Specify the amount of funding required (if seeking investment or loans) and the purpose of the funds.

_____

_____

_____

_____

_____

_____

_____

_____

- Use of Funds: Clearly state how the funding will be utilized to grow and enhance your box truck business.

_____

_____

_____

_____

_____

_____

- Repayment Plan: Include a repayment plan for investors or lenders, demonstrating your commitment to timely repayments.

_____

_____

_____

_____

_____

Remember, your business plan is a living document that should evolve with your business. Regularly review and update it as you make progress and adapt to changing market conditions. A well-crafted business plan will serve as a roadmap, guiding your box truck business toward long-term success and profitability.

FINANCIAL PROJECTIONS TEMPLATE

Note: *The following template provides a framework to help you create financial projections for your box truck business over the next three to five years. Customize and expand each section based on your specific business model and market conditions.*

1. Sales Revenue Projections

Year	Month 1	Month 2	Month 3	Month 4
Year 1	$	$	$	$
Year 2	$	$	$	$
Year 3	$	$	$	$
Year 4	$	$	$	$
Year 5	$	$	$	$

Year	Month 5	Month 6	Month 7	Month 8
Year 1	$	$	$	$
Year 2	$	$	$	$
Year 3	$	$	$	$
Year 4	$	$	$	$
Year 5	$	$	$	$

Year	Month 9	Month 10	Month 11	Month 12
Year 1	$	$	$	$
Year 2	$	$	$	$
Year 3	$	$	$	$
Year 4	$	$	$	$
Year 5	$	$	$	$

3. Operating Expenses

Expense Category	Year 1	Year 2	Year 3	Year 4	Year 5	Year 6
Salaries and Wages						
Rent/Lease						
Insurance						
Maintenance and Repairs						
Fuel						
Marketing and Advertising						
Administrative Expenses						
Other Expenses						
Total Operating Expenses						

4. Gross Profit

Year	Gross Profit
Year 1	
Year 2	
Year 3	
Year 4	

Year 5	

5. Net Income Before Tax

Year	Net Income Before Tax
Year 1	
Year 2	
Year 3	
Year 4	
Year 5	

6. Cash Flow Projection

Year	Cash Inflow	Cash Outflow	Net Cash Flow
Year 1			
Year 2			
Year 3			
Year 4			
Year 5			

7. Break-Even Analysis

Year	Break-Even Sales (Revenue)
Year 1	
Year 2	
Year 3	
Year 4	
Year 5	

8. Financial Ratios

Year	Current Ratio	Debt-to-Equity Ratio	Gross Profit Margin (%)	Net Profit Margin (%)
Year 1				
Year 2				
Year 3				
Year 4				
Year 5				

Note: Provide formulas used to calculate financial ratios, if necessary.

Conclusion:

The Financial Projections Template will help you forecast your box truck business's financial performance, enabling you to make informed decisions and set achievable goals. Use this template as a tool to assess the financial health of your business over the next few years and adjust your strategies accordingly. Remember to revisit and update these projections regularly to reflect changes in the market and the growth of your business. With accurate financial projections, you can steer your box truck business toward long-term success and financial stability.

MARKETING STRATEGIES TEMPLATE

Note: The Marketing Strategies Template will assist you in crafting a comprehensive marketing plan for your box truck business. Customize each section to align with your specific business model and target market.

1. Executive Summary

- **Business Overview:** Provide a brief overview of your box truck business, highlighting its mission, products/services, and unique selling points.

_____

_____

_____

_____

_____

_____

_____

_____

- **Marketing Goals:** State the specific marketing objectives you aim to achieve, such as increasing brand awareness, attracting new customers, or boosting sales.

_____

_____

_____

_____

_____

_____

_____

_____

2. Target Market Analysis

- Target Audience: Describe your ideal customer profile, including demographics, location, interests, and purchasing behavior.

_____

_____

_____

_____

_____

_____

- Customer Pain Points: Identify the challenges or needs your target audience faces that your box truck services can address.

_____

_____

_____

_____

_____

_____

_____

_____

3. Branding and Positioning

- Brand Identity: Define your brand identity, including the brand name, logo, color scheme, and tagline that align with your box truck business's values and image.

_____

_____

_____

_____

_____

_____

_____

_____

_____

_____

_____

_____

_____

_____

_____

- Brand Positioning: Explain how you want your brand to be perceived in the market and what sets your business apart from competitors.

_____

_____

_____

_____

_____

_____

_____

_____

4. Marketing Channels and Tactics

- Online Marketing:
  - Website: Describe your website and its purpose, ensuring it is user-friendly, visually appealing, and optimized for search engines.

_____

_____

_____

_____

_____

_____

_____

  - Social Media: Identify the social media platforms you will use to connect with your target audience, outlining content strategies and posting schedules.

_____

_____

_____

_____

_____

_____

_____

- Email Marketing: Detail your email marketing campaigns, including lead generation, newsletters, and promotional offers.

_____

_____

_____

_____

_____

_____

_____

_____

- Online Advertising: Discuss your plans for online advertising, such as Google Ads or social media ads, to reach a broader audience.

_____

_____

_____

_____

_____

_____

_____

_____

- Offline Marketing:
  - Local Events: Mention your participation in local events, trade shows, or community gatherings to increase brand visibility.

_____

_____

_____

_____

_____

_____

_____

  - Flyers and Brochures: Outline the distribution of physical marketing materials in strategic locations to attract local customers.

_____

_____

_____

_____

_____

_____

_____

_____

- Networking: Explain how you will network with potential clients and industry partners to generate leads and referrals.

_____

_____

_____

_____

_____

_____

_____

5. Content Marketing Strategy

- Content Creation: Describe the types of content you will create to engage and educate your audience, such as blog posts, videos, infographics, or case studies.

_____

_____

_____

_____

_____

_____

_____

_____

_____

_____

- Content Distribution: Outline how you will share your content through various channels, maximizing its reach and impact.

_____

_____

_____

_____

_____

_____

_____

6. Customer Relationship Management (CRM)

- Customer Support: Detail your customer support system, ensuring prompt response to inquiries and issues.

_____

_____

_____

_____

_____

_____

_____

_____

- Loyalty Programs: Discuss any loyalty programs or customer rewards to encourage repeat business and foster customer loyalty.

_____

_____

_____

_____

_____

_____

_____

_____

7. Budget Allocation

- **Marketing Budget:** Allocate funds for each marketing activity and channel, ensuring a balanced distribution of resources for optimal results.

_____

_____

_____

_____

_____

_____

8. Marketing Timeline and Milestones

- **Marketing Calendar:** Create a timeline that highlights key marketing activities and milestones, ensuring a structured and organized approach.

_____

_____

_____

_____

_____

_____

_____

_____

- Evaluation and Adjustment: Plan regular evaluations of your marketing strategies' performance and make necessary adjustments based on feedback and results.

_____

_____

_____

_____

_____

_____

_____

Conclusion:

The Marketing Strategies Template is a powerful tool to guide your marketing efforts for your box truck business. By customizing and implementing the strategies outlined in this template, you can effectively reach your target audience, enhance brand awareness, and generate quality leads. Remember to measure the success of your marketing initiatives regularly and adapt your strategies as needed to achieve sustainable growth and success in the competitive box truck industry. A well-executed marketing plan will play a vital role in establishing your business as a trusted and sought-after transportation solution in the market.

Attribution

All images used in this book were downloaded from *pexels.com* & *pixabay.com*

Made in the USA
Columbia, SC
22 January 2024

30780216R00065